MOZA

his greatest
PIANO SOLOS

A Comprehensive Collection Of His World Famous Works

Preludes

Minuets

Rondos

Fantasias

Piano Recreations

Sonatas

Variations

IN THEIR ORIGINAL FORM

Compiled by
ALEXANDER SHEALY

Sole selling agent: **ASHLEY DEALERS SERVICE** • 263 Veterans Blvd., Carlstadt, N. J. 07072

CONTENTS

K = Köchel Index

WOLFGANG AMADEUS MOZART

(Pronounced Mote-zart)

Born Salzburg, Austria, January 27, 1756

Died Vienna, Austria, December 15, 1792

Wolfgang Amadeus Mozart was the son of Leopold Mozart, an accomplished musician (violinist, composer and chapel master at the court of the Archbishop of Salzburg). Wolfgang showed promise as an infant and composed little pieces when he was only four. His father gave music lessons both to Wolfgang and to his somewhat older sister, Marianne. When he was only six years old, his father decided to take him and his sister on concert tours. The boy's genius aroused great enthusiasm. By the time he was 16, he took part in concerts in leading European cities.

When in Italy, he was inspired to compose (later in Vienna) three operas which were destined for world wide acclaim, Don Giovanni, The Marriage of Figaro and The Magic Flute.

Mozart was married in 1782 to Constance Weber of Munich. They had six children, but only two survived his own premature death.

In spite of ill health and poverty (having been cheated out of his profits from his successful operatic works), he composed over 600 works in his short life span. He goes into history as one of the world's greatest composers of all time. Outstanding among his masterpieces are the Requiem (commissioned by one Count Walseck in memory of his dead wife), a dozen great symphonies, fifteen brilliant piano concertos, music for string quintets, sonatas, sonatinas, rondos and minuets.

All of Mozart's works reveal perfection in craftsmanship and a seemingly endless flow of creative melody in a great variety of moods.

This illustration reproduces a copper medallion (now at the Mozart exhibit in Munich). The medallion was made in 1789 by a contemporary artist, Ludwig Posch, and was a gift from Mozart to Beethoven.

MOZART'S PIANO

WOLFGANG at piano with MARIA ANNA (1751-1829), his sister. Holding violin, his father LEOPOLD MOZART (1719-1829). Wolfgang's mother, Anna Maria nee Pertl, is in framed picture.

ALLA TURCA

(Turkish March from Sonata in A)

WOLFGANG AMADEUS MOZART

Allegretto

cresc.
ten.
ten.

p
mp
p
cresc.
fzp
f
1.
2.
ff

f
p
più
sff

EINE KLEINE NACHTMUSIC

(A Little Night Music)

I. ROMANCE

WOLFGANG AMADEUS MOZART

1.
2.
mf
mf
cresc.
f
1.
2.
mf
più f
f
dim. poco a poco
rall.
p a tempo

cresc.
dim.
mp
(tr)
mf
Più mosso
mf
f
1
mf

rall. e dim.
Come Prima
(tr)
1.
2.

rall. e dim.
mp a tempo
f
p
rall. e dim.
pp

EINE KLEINE NACHTMUSIC

(A Little Night Music)

WOLFGANG AMADEUS MOZART

II. RONDO

f
p
f

f
p
f
p
f

Coda
p
tr
tr
f

EINE KLEINE NACHTMUSIC

(A Little Night Music)

III. ALLEGRO

WOLFGANG AMADEUS MOZART

tr
p
sf
cresc.
f

MINUET

(From "Don Giovanni")

Moderato

WOLFGANG AMADEUS MOZART

f
mf
mf

MINUET

(From SYMPHONY IN E♭)

WOLFGANG AMADEUS MOZART

mf
p
f-p
f

p
p
f
pp
TRIO
cantando
p

espressione
pp
mf
p
mf
p
p
p

f-p
f
f
mf
p
mf
p
p
p
f
pp

MINUET

(From "Linz" Symphony)

WOLFGANG AMADEUS MOZART

FANTASIA IN C MINOR

(No. 1)

WOLFGANG AMADEUS MOZART

mf
p
semplice
mfz
f
dim.
f
dim.
espr.
p
espr.
espr.
dimin.
dimin.
pp

ten.
sosten.
(tr)
p cresc.
tr
cresc.
cresc.
dim.
simile
tr
dolce
espr.
dolce
pp
poco marcato

simile
cresc. (poco)
dim. e rit.
a tempo
p
leggiero
pp espr.
cresc.
dim.
fp
mf
mfz
pp
f
più f

string. - - - rall.
cresc. - - -
fz
f
dim.
p
Agitato
mf
f
dim.
cresc.
f
dim.
cresc.
f
sempre f

ffz p
pesante
fz p
pesante
dim.
mfz p
pesante
fz p
fz
cresc.
fz

f
più f
ff
Basso marcato
ad lib.
dim.
pp
Tempo I

p cresc.
fz
f
p
mf
f
dim.
p
dim.
poco cresc.
mf
p
f
dim.
p

espr.
cresc.
espr.
espr.
dimin.
f
p
f
p
f
p cresc.
dim.
p
dolce
espr.
dolce

pp
simile
poco cresc.
string
rit.
dim.
tranquillo
p
leggiero
espr.
fp
fz
cantabile

FANTASIA IN D MINOR

WOLFGANG AMADEUS MOZART

cresc.
Presto
l.h.
Tempo I
cresc.
cresc.
cresc.

Presto
f
p
Tempo I
p
pp
f
sf
p
pp
fp
f
cresc.
accelerando
fz
a tempo
Allegretto
p
mp dolce
p
1.
2.
mp

NOTE: A NEW AND COMPLETE CATALOG OF CENTURY EDITION IS ISSUED EACH SEASON. PLEASE ASK YOUR DEALER FOR A COPY IT IS FREE— THE PUBLISHERS.

SONATA FACILE
IN C

WOLFGANG AMADEUS MOZART

a) Original: b) c) Original: c)

(rinf.)
d)
C
D
(f)
d)

e) 

f) Original: 

cresc.
F
mfp
(legato)
sf
g)
f
(rinf.)
h)
G
g)
g) Original:
h)

Andante. (♩= 84)

a) Original:

C
(rinf.)
(rinf.)
(rinf.)
D
Ped.

dolce
(rinf.)
mfp
(rinf.)
f
E
p
sf
(rinf.)
f cresc.
sf
sf
sf
p
(più p)
Rondo
follows

Rondo.

Allegretto (♪= 120)

a) Original:

E
p
(rinf.)
(rinf.)
f
(legato)
cresc.
F
poco f
f
G
mf
(legato)
sf
f
mf
sf
f
H
ff
Ped.

MENUETTO IN F

Allegretto moderato

WOLFGANG AMADEUS MOZART

SONATA IN B FLAT

WOLFGANG AMADEUS MOZART

Allegro

f
a)
fz
fz p
tr
b)
c)
fz
p
fz p
d)
f
e) tr
f
a)
b)
c)
d)
e)

sf
sf
f
sf
sf
f
f
ten.
ten.
p
f
p
cresc.
f
cresc.
f
tr
p
tr

cresc.
p cresc.
dim.

cresc.
fz
fz
dim.
p
poco rit.
a tempo
mf
p
f
p
f

p
decres - cen - do
p
a)
fz p
fz p
tr
fz p
a)

fz
f
tr
sf
sf
f
sf
sf
f
ten.
ten.
p
f
p

cresc.
f
a)
p
cresc.
f
p
cresc.
f
p
a)

ADAGIO

WOLFGANG AMADEUS MOZART

ARIETTA

WOLFGANG AMADEUS MOZART

RONDO ALLEGRO

Allegro

WOLFGANG AMADEUS MOZART

* tr = ~

VARIATIONS ON A FRENCH FOLK SONG

("Ah, Vous Dirai-je, Maman")

Theme

WOLFGANG AMADEUS MOZART

Var. II

Var. III

Var. IV
f
p
cresc.
f
Var. V
p
mf
dimin.
p
Var. VI
p
legato
cresc.
al
f

cresc.
al
cresc.
al
Var. VII

Var. VIII

Var. XI
Adagio
cresc.

 Var. XII

Allegro

LULLABY

WOLFGANG AMADEUS MOZART

Andante

CONCERTO No. 21

(Theme)

WOLFGANG AMADEUS MOZART

sempre espressivo
mf
Ped.
dim.
dolce
f
tr
4323

dolce
poco cresc.
mf
f

dim.
dolce
mf
f
p
pp
Ped.

MENUETTO IN D

WOLFGANG AMADEUS MOZART

Moderato

dolce
mancando
f
p
f
p
f
p
f
p
p

CAPRICCIO

WOLFGANG AMADEUS MOZART

tr
tr

Andantino
Presto
Adagio
Andantino
tr
Cantabile
Allegro
p
crescendo
fp
p
crescendo
f
p
tr
f
p
CAPRICCIO
Allegro

tr
Presto
ff

GAVOTTE

Allegro

WOLFGANG AMADEUS MOZART

p
f
Coda

ADAGIO IN B MINOR

WOLFGANG AMADEUS MOZART

p sf p sf sfp p f p f
p sf p sf p sf p p
sf p sf p p sf sfp p f p
f p mf p mf p mf p
f p f p

f
p
f
f

MARCH FUNEBRE

(Funeral March)

WOLFGANG AMADEUS MOZART

Adagio

PRELUDE IN C

WOLFGANG AMADEUS MOZART

fz
fz
Piu adagio

Tempo I
p
pp

FUGUE

Andante maestoso

Adagio

ALLEGRO

(From "JUPITER SYMPHONY" No. 49)

WOLFGANG AMADEUS MOZART

Allegro vivaci

cresc.
cresc.
Ped.

Ped.
f
sf
p
sempre f

GAVOTTE

(Ballet "Les Petits Riens")

WOLFGANG AMADEUS MOZART

ANDANTE

Andante

WOLFGANG AMADEUS MOZART

LARGHETTO

Larghetto

WOLFGANG AMADEUS MOZART

GIGUE

WOLFGANG AMADEUS MOZART

POLONAISE

WOLFGANG AMADEUS MOZART

Allegretto

THE MARRIAGE OF FIGARO

OVERTURE

WOLFGANG AMADEUS MOZART

ff
f
p
f
p

f
p
f

fp
fp
fp
fp
fp
fp
p
fp
fp
fp
fp
fp
fp
f
p
f
p

f
f
p

f
p
f
p
f
p
f
p
f
p
f
p
f
p
pp

p
ff
p

tr
f
fp
fp
fp
fp
fp
p
fp
fp
fp
fp
fp
fp

p
f
p
f
p
f
p
f
p

tr
3
3
pp

cresc.
f
tr

tr
tr

ARIA

(From "THE MARRIAGE OF FIGARO")

Marcato

WOLFGANG AMADEUS MOZART

SONATA XVI

THEME

WOLFGANG AMADEUS MOZART

Andante grazioso

NOTE. - Also see "ALLA TURCA" (Turkish March from the same SONATA), page 6.

f
Ped.
tr
p
fz
cresc.
dim.

Var. II

p
cresc.
f
Var. III (♪ = 112)
Minore
p espress.
mf
sempre legato

Var. IV (♪= 120)
Maggiore
m.g.
Ped.

Var. V
Adagio (♪= 60)
p espress.
cresc.
dim.
Ped.

ten.
ten.
a)
cresc.
dim.

Var. VI

Allegro

Menuetto (♩ = 116)

cresc.
Ped.
cresc.
Ped.

Trio

Menuetto D.C.

CONCERT RONDO

WOLFGANG AMADEUS MOZART

Allegretto grazioso

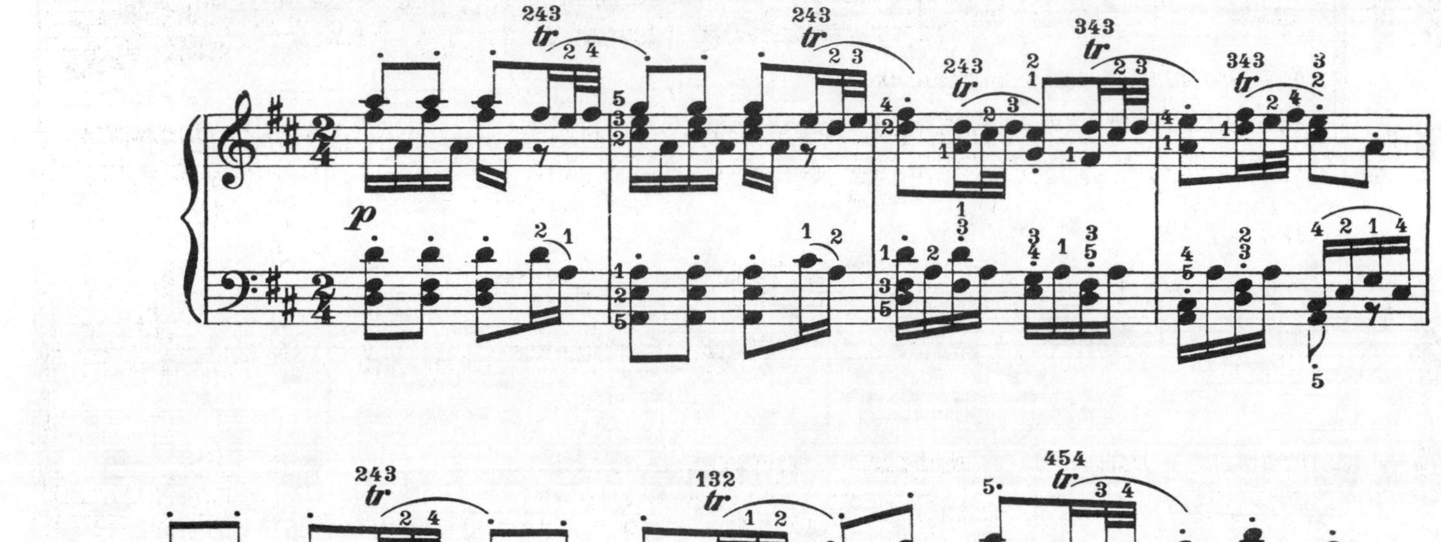

p espressivo e sempre grazioso
legato
Ped. ad lib.
fp
mf
tr

tr
mf legato
p
legato
mf
cresc.
f
p

tr
p espressivo
mf
p
pp
una corda
f
tre corde

Adagio
p dolce espressivo
sfp
mf
f
dolce

Allegro ♩. = 80

cresc.

pp
f
Ped.
mf
sf
f
p
f
sf
sf
sf
f
tr
rit.
p
l.h.

TEMPO I Allegretto grazioso

SONATINA

Andante

WOLFGANG AMADEUS MOZART

FANTASIA IN C MINOR

(No. 2)

WOLFGANG AMADEUS MOZART

ten.
Ped.
dim.
cresc.
poco cresc.
più cresc.
calando
cresc.

Ped.
cresc.

Allegro (♩ = 144)
f
mf
p
mp
sf
espress.
Ped.
cresc.
Ped.

cresc.
cresc. poco a poco.
poco rit.
Allegro
poco rit.

fz
rallent.
Andantino (♩ = 52)
p
f
p
cresc.
f
p
p
f
p
cresc.
mf
f
p
mp
p
f
p
cresc.

cresc.
Ped.
Più allegro (♩= 66)
il basso marcato

Ped.
Ped.
Ped.
Ped.
dim.
mf

decresc.
Ped.
L.H.
cresc.
rall.
Tempo primo

poco cresc.
più cresc.
cresc.
poco cresc.
cresc.
più cresc.

GLOCKENSPIEL

(From "THE MAGIC FLUTE")

WOLFGANG AMADEUS MOZART

Allegro moderato

ARIA

(From "DON GIOVANNI")

WOLFGANG AMADEUS MOZART

Andantino

SONATA IN C MINOR

WOLFGANG AMADEUS MOZART

Molto allegro

cantabile
cresc.
cresc.
dim.
Ped.
Ped.

calando

Ped.
Ped.
Ped.
Ped.
Ped.
Ped.

cresc.
cresc.

cresc.
Ped.
dim.

Adagio
sotto voce
f
p
cresc.
f
p
cresc.
f
p
cresc.
f
p
cresc.
f
p
p
p
Ped.
cresc.
mf
p
mf

dimin.
più cresc.
mancando
cresc.
Ped.

cresc.
fp
cresc.
f
p
p
cresc.
p
cresc.
f
p
cresc.
p
f
p
Ped.
Ped.
f
p
fp
fp
fp
cresc.
Ped.

cresc.
cresc.
calando e poco rit.

a tempo
cresc.
cresc.
cresc.

cresc.
p
fp
fp
p
cresc.
dim.
p
cresc.
d)
f
poco rit.

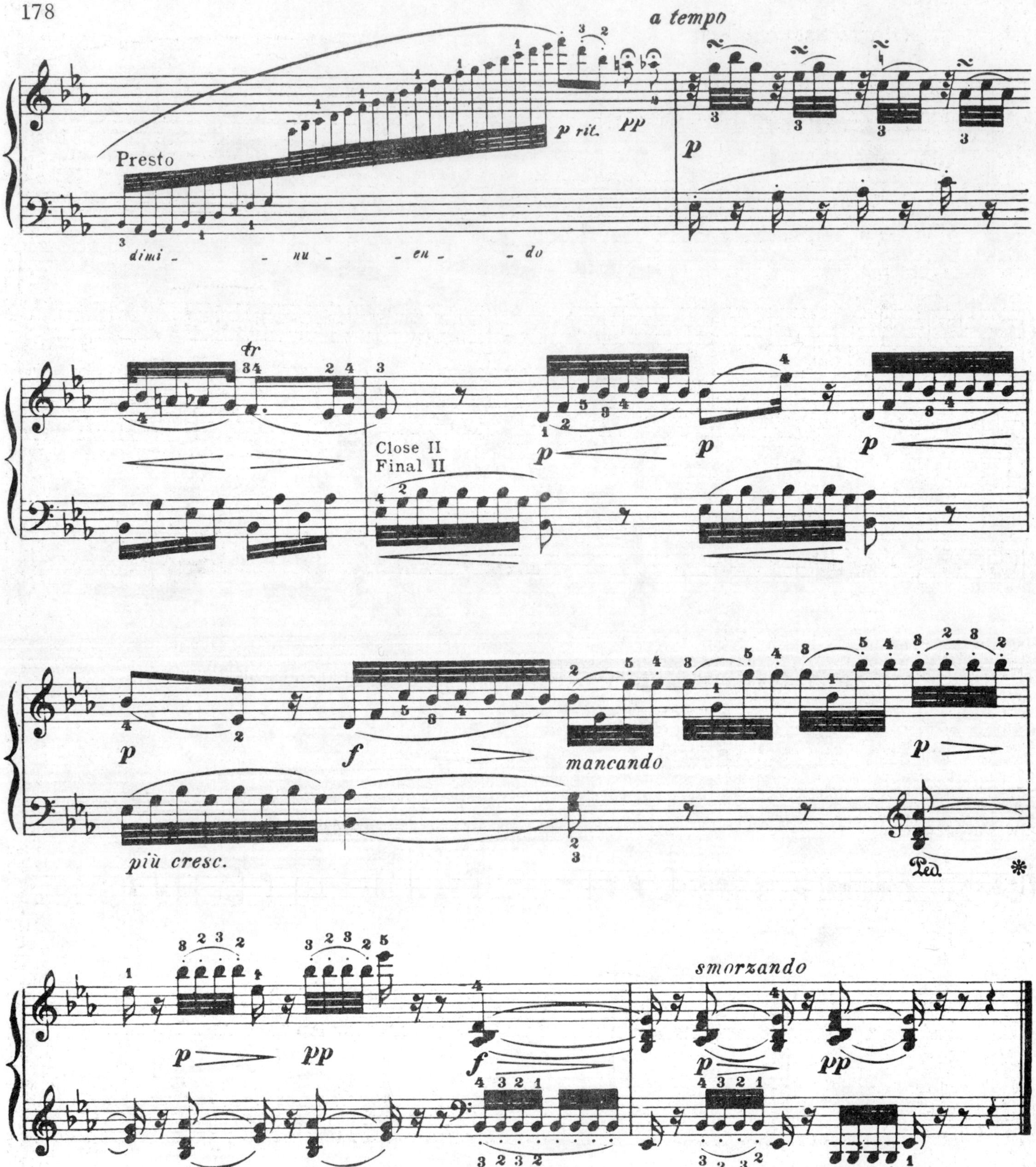
a tempo
Presto
p rit.
pp
dimi - nu - en - do
p
tr
Close II
Final II
p
p
p
più cresc.
f
mancando
p
Ped.
p
pp
Ped.
Ped.
f
smorzando
p
pp

Allegro assai (𝅗𝅥. = 66)

con espress.
cresc.
cresc.

mf
sempre cresc.
Ped.
f
p
cresc.
mf
fz
ff
un poco espress.

p
fp
Ped.
p
mp
cresc.
p
cresc.
f
p
p
f
mf
ff
p
Ped.
fp
fp
fp
fp
fp
p
fp
fp
fp

fp
cresc.
f
Ped.
p
a piacere (più lento)
a tempo
più cresc.
pp
fz
ff

ff
p
f
p
cresc.
decresc.
f
p
mf
sempre p
ff

SYMPHONY No. 40 IN G MINOR

(1st Movement)

WOLFGANG AMADEUS MOZART

Allegro molto

cresc.

non legato

Ped.
Ped.

cresc.